GENERAL
ERCHANDISE

Wyatt Earp's West

Wyatt Earp's West

Images and Words

Photographs by Ben Glass

Text Selected by Jim Wilson

Foreword by Page Stegner

Newmarket Press

New York

Credits and acknowledgments of permissions for text from other works are found on page 108.

This book published simultaneously in the United States of America and in Canada.

94 95 96 97 10 9 8 7 6 5 4 3 2 1

Library of Congress Cataloging-in-Publication Data
Glass, Ben.
Wyatt Earp's West: Images and Words/photographs by Ben Glass.
p. cm.
ISBN 1-55704-199-7
1. Wyatt Earp (Motion picture) I. Title.
PN1997.W93 1994b
791.43'72—dc20 94-7932 CIP

Quantity Purchases
Companies, professional groups, clubs, and other organizations may qualify for special terms when ordering quantities of this title. For information, write Special Sales Department, Newmarket Press, 18 East 48th Street, New York, NY 10017, or call (212) 832-3575.

Produced by Newmarket Productions, a division of Newmarket Publishing & Communications Company: Esther Margolis, director, Keith Hollaman, editor, Joe Gannon, production manager, Grace Farrell, assistant editor.

Book design by Tania Garcia

Manufactured in Japan
First Edition

Other Newmarket Pictorial Moviebooks include:
The Age of Innocence: A Portrait of the Film Based on the Novel by Edith Wharton
Bram Stoker's Dracula: The Film and the Legend
City of Joy: The Illustrated Story of the Film
Dances With Wolves: The Illustrated Story of the Epic Film
Far and Away: The Illustrated Story of a Journey from Ireland to America in the 1890s
Gandhi: A Pictorial Biography
The Inner Circle: An Inside View of Soviet Life Under Stalin
Last Action Hero: The Official Moviebook
Neil Simon's Lost in Yonkers: The Illustrated Screenplay of the Film
Rapa Nui: The Easter Island Legend on Film
Wyatt Earp: The Film and the Filmmakers

To my parents, Leslie and Henry Glass

—BG

To my family, Theresa, Lauren, and Maeve

—JW

Foreword

Looking at this collection of Ben Glass photographs, shot in New Mexico during the filming of *Wyatt Earp*, I am impressed by many things, among them the durability of cowboy and gunslinger myths, and the national addiction to a genre that has relatively little to do with the real settling of the American West. Like most people I love the illusion of wildness and freedom, of wide open spaces, of an endless frontier; I cheer for those macho hombres proving their manhood with fast draws and ox-stunning fisticuffs; I lust after those pulchritudinous females in the shadowy corners of smokey saloons; I even commiserate with those docile sweethearts back at the ranch who fail to understand that a show of courage in the face of death is a far higher calling than domesticity.

These pictures remind me, too, of the way in which a camera lens focused on specific, carefully orchestrated aspects of the physical environment—say, a vast, empty prairie sporting nothing but a solitary, distant rider on the horizon, or a tiny railroad train stitching along like an ant column across a colossal, foreground desert, backdropped by an equally enormous and vacant sky—can create the illusion of time unaltered. "Environment" is as essential to a Western film as the horse and six-gun, and the symbiotic relationship between man and nature represented in great landscape shots seems to me the most authentic union one can describe in a visual depiction of the American West. The stark, often violent, harshness of an arid land is a perfect metaphor for the poor, struggling humans who attempt to survive in it.

The other major issue that strikes me as I look through this volume is the remarkable changes in phototechnology that enable an artist like Ben Glass to do what he does. There may be a stylistic similarity to early photographs of the region, but it is hard to imagine what pioneer image-makers like Charles Savage, Carleton Watkins, William Bell, Timothy O'Sullivan, and William Henry Jackson might say to Glass were he to tell them (as producer Jim Wilson tells us in his introduction) that he took twenty-five thousand pictures during the five months of filming. Early photographers used wet, glass plates, which had to be meticulously cleaned, coated with collodion, sensitized in a bath of silver nitrate, exposed, and then immediately developed (an equally cumbersome process involving rinsing, fixing, rinsing again, drying, and varnishing); they were lucky to make seven or eight exposures a day.

And what would Eadweard Muybridge (1830–1904) think of images of horses running full tilt through a Wyoming canyon, or of riders flying through mid-air as their mounts are shot out from under them? Muybridge was the first to figure out how to photograph a *moving* subject, and, indeed, came up with an invention called the magic-lantern zoetrope, a gizmo that produced, in 1879, the first reconstruction of *continuous* space-time motion (in short, a precursor to the moving picture). But motor drive cameras? 5.7 frames per second? 1/500 exposure times? In order to photograph *his* object in motion (a galloping horse) Muybridge had to use twelve cameras placed about two feet apart, with strings attached to their shutter mechanisms, and he had to rely on the horse to trip the shutters as it thundered down a race track. So when Jim Wilson alludes in his introduction to a stuntman being shot through a saloon window and Ben Glass's photographs catching, at one five-hundredth of a second, the shards of flying glass as they fall, he is not only reminding us that while a re-creation of Wyatt Earp's West can logistically be made to appear very authentic, the capacity to record its revitalization is very much a circumstance of our own time.

Page Stegner

Santa Cruz, California

Introduction

As a producer of *Wyatt Earp* I was fortunate enough to look at the twenty-five thousand or so still photographs taken by Ben Glass during our five months of filming in and around Sante Fe, New Mexico. From mid-July to mid-December 1993 our cast and crew worked six days a week to bring *Earp* to the screen.

As the film's unit photographer, Ben was responsible for capturing our epic motion picture with his still camera. Each morning bright and early, as the sun hiked up the Sangre De Cristo mountains, I would see Ben preparing for his day. I could always find him because his dog Sage (half coyote, half God only knows) would be making the rounds. Ben was knee-deep in lenses, filters, cameras, and, worst of all, film. I told him he had to shoot less, because he was going overbudget. He simply looked at me and said, "I can't," and headed off to the scene of the crime. There wasn't much I could do. It would have been like taking canvas away from a painter or marble from a sculptor.

The vast majority of the stills featured our stars—and we had our share of stars—in their most glamorous moments to be used by the studio for publicity purposes down the line. As I searched for the top fifty publicity shots, I found dozens of others that moved me not as publicity shots but as interesting photos. Some were mere silhouettes against a dusty road, others depicted action scenes frozen in time; some were in black and white, most were in color. But they all touched a nerve, so Ben and I thought we should present these photographs in a more formal way, hence, *Wyatt Earp's West*.

In real time, these shots took the camera about one collective second to record, and yet more than a year of preparation and execution by hundreds of people are reflected in them. Each one of these pictures is a collaboration of actors, directors, lighting technicians, designers, costumers, wranglers, and others. Each shot brings back to life for me the very moment of filming, that split second when the movie magic happens.

Everyone knows movies are artifice but they become very real to those who make them. We built the towns, clothed the cast, rode the wagons, ate the food, and spoke the talk. We went back in time more than one hundred and twenty years, and whether it was the shootout at the OK Corral or the building of the transcontinental railroad, we re-created it. These photos are proof.

As a subject matter I find Westerns particularly fascinating to shoot. First, I enjoy being outdoors and interacting with nature. Many of these photographs are influenced by the wide array of light and expansive landscapes that New Mexico has to offer. During our twenty-one weeks, the sun's path changed dramatically and the seasons turned from hot and dusty to cold and muddy. In short, we had to deal with the elements, and they made their presence known in each and every shot.

Second, Westerns portray a time when people seemed much more independent and more adventuresome. Ben's photos capture the drama of the journey west and the vitality of frontier life and celebrate these vanishing qualities. Finally, Westerns always have a shoot-out or two, and *Wyatt Earp* is no exception. What I have always wanted to do is slow down the action or stop it altogether, so I could examine a particular moment in time more closely. For instance, there is a scene in *Wyatt Earp* in which Ed Masterson blows a guy through a window, and the shards of glass fall all around him while dozens of bar patrons scatter to the wind. I want to see what the naked eye and the motion picture camera cannot: that one five-hundredth of a second upon impact that only Ben's camera can capture. We have selected many of those moments for you.

Along with the photos we have included an eclectic collection of poetry, stories, sayings, and quotes that I ran across while doing research for the movie. Some are a bit verbose, others are silly, and still others are scholarly and to the point. But like the photos, they all struck a nerve. We tried to include material that would augment the pictures and help them tell a more complete story. I hope we have succeeded.

On a more selfish note, I did not take along a still camera of my own during production. I feel a bit self-conscious snapping shots and producing at the same time. So while helping to create this book I was given a chance to look back upon what was a glorious time in my life and recall many an afternoon spent in New Mexico among my friends. In truth it's much like a family album since all members of the cast and crew end up being like brothers, sisters, aunts, and uncles. I suspect as I grow older I will saunter to the bookshelf, extract my copy, and leaf through these images remembering this chapter in my life with real affection. Remembering the Old West, as they say.

Jim Wilson

March 1994

Wyatt Earp's West

It was still the Wild West in those days, the Far West, the West of Owen Wister's stories and Frederic Remington's drawings, the West of Indian and the buffalo-hunter, the soldier and the cow-puncher. That land of the West has gone now, "gone, gone with lost Atlantis," gone to the isle of ghosts and of strange dead memories. It was a land of vast and silent spaces, of lonely rivers, and of plains where the wild game stared at the passing horseman. It was a land of scattered ranches, of herds of long-horned cattle, and of reckless riders who unmoved looked in the eyes of death. In that land we led a free and hardy life, with horse and with rifle. We worked under the scorching midsummer sun, when the wide plains shimmered and wavered in the heat; and we knew the freezing misery of riding night guard round the cattle in the late fall round-up. In the soft springtime the stars were glorious in our eyes each night before we fell asleep; and in the winter we rode through blinding blizzards, when the driven snow-dust burnt our faces. There were monotonous days, as we guided the trail cattle or the beef herds, hour after hour, at the slowest of walks; and minutes or hours teeming with excitement as we stopped stampedes or swam the herds across rivers treacherous with quicksands or brimmed with running ice. We knew toil and hardship and hunger and thirst; and we saw men die violent deaths as they worked among the horses and cattle, or fought in evil feuds, with one another; but we felt the beat of hardy life in our veins, and ours was the glory of work and the joy of living.

—Theodore Roosevelt

O you youths, Western youths,
So impatient, full of action, full of manly pride and friendship,
Plain I see you Western youths, see you trampling with the foremost,
Pioneers! O pioneers!

All the past we leave behind,
We debouch upon a new and mightier world, varied world,
Fresh and strong the world we seize, world of labor and the march,
Pioneers! O pioneers!

We detachments steady throwing,
Down the edges, through the passes, up the mountains steep,
Conquering, holding, daring, venturing as we go the unknown ways,
Pioneers! O pioneers!

On and on the compact ranks,
With accessions ever waiting, with the places of the dead quickly fill'd,
Through the battle, through defeat, moving yet and never stopping,
Pioneers! O pioneers!

All the pulses of the world,
Falling in they beat for us, with the Western movement beat,
Holding single or together, steady moving to the front, all for us,
Pioneers! O pioneers!

—Walt Whitman, "Pioneers! O Pioneers!"

A description of life on the trail by Jesse Applegate, leader of a "cow-column" for slower wagons and herds:

Sentinels fired their rifles at four o'clock in the morning to wake the camp. Fires were lighted and the herders drove the oxen into the circle of wagons to be yoked for the day's journey. This corral of the plains was made the night before by parking the wagons in a circle. The rear wagon was connected with the wagon in front by its tongue and ox chains. It was strong enough to keep the oxen from breaking out, and also served as a barricade in case of an Indian attack.

Five to seven o'clock were busy hours, with breakfast to be eaten, teams yolked, tents folded and wagons loaded. Promptly at seven the bugle sounded, and the wagon train was on its way. Women and children often walked beside the trail, gathering wild flowers and odd-looking stones. Boys and young men on horseback kept the loose stock from straying too far, as they trailed along behind the wagons. At noon the emigrants stopped to eat. Oxen were turned loose with their yokes on, so they might graze and rest. Sometimes the officers of the train got together at noon to consider the case of someone who had violated the rules or had commited a crime. He was given a fair trial and, if found guilty, was sentenced according to the nature of his offense.

At one o'clock the bugle sounded, and the wagons were once more on their way. All through the afternoon the oxen plodded, and when the wagons arrived at the spot chosen by the guide as a camping place, preparations were made to spend the night. Livestock were driven out to pasture, tents were pitched, fires built, and supper was on its way. Perhaps hunters came in with choice parts of a buffalo or antelope, and everyone enjoyed a feast.

After supper, the children played their favorite games; the elders gathered in groups and talked, perhaps making plans for the new homes to be built at the end of the trail. Some of the young folk danced to the music of fiddle or accordion; while those more seriously minded sang their favorite songs, some religious, some sentimental....But youth was not to be denied, the trek was a great adventure, and life stretched far ahead.

—Howard R. Driggs, *The Old West Speaks*

You got to cross that lonesome valley,
You got to cross hit by yo'self,
They hain't no one goin cross hit for you.

—Stephen Longstreet, *The Wilder Shore*

One of the most notorious stage coach robbers of the old West was Black Bart. He operated for over eight years without being caught, pulling off more than thirty robberies without ever firing a shot, his gun was never loaded. He never robbed a passenger, taking only the Wells Fargo treasure box. After emptying the box he would leave it with some verse, always signed Black Bart Po8. The notorious Black Bart proved to be Charles E. Boles, a high-class, educated, middle-class man, who had been a Union officer in the Civil War and in the early 1870s found himself teaching school in the northern mines before turning to a life of crime.

—G. Ezra Dane,
Ghost Town

DAILY REPORTER
WICHITA BANK
AMBULANCE

Wichita sprawled in the dust and mud on her river-bank as unattractively as any Kansas settlement of the decade. Sidewalks of plank or of heel-tamped clay ran underneath the inevitable wooden awnings which stretched from the ludicrously false facades of stores and saloons to shade the loafers' benches; post was linked to post at the curblines by cayuse-cribbed hitching-rails.

As Wyatt first saw her, Wichita was merely another Kansas cowcamp, with longer streets, more stores, saloons, gambling-houses, and honky-tonks, larger crowds of cowboys, and, by these tokens, more trouble.

—Stuart Lake, *Wyatt Earp, Frontier Marshal*

We're the children of the open and we hate the haunts o' men,
  But we had to come to town to get the mail.
And we're riding' home at daybreak — 'cause the air is cooler then —
  All 'cept one of us that stopped behind in jail.
Shorty's nose won't bear paradin', Bill's off eye is darkly fadin',
  All our toilets show a touch of disarray;
For we found that City life is a constant round of strife,
  And we ain't the breed for shyin' from a fray.

Chant your war-whoops, pardners dear, while the east turns pale with fear,
  And the chaparral is tremblin' all aroun';
For we're wicked to the marrer; we're a midnight dream of terror,
  When we're ridin' up the rocky trail from town!

— Badger Clark

TOMBST E BANK
WELLS FARG
WELLS FA

Some came for lungs, and some for jobs,
And some for booze at Big-mouth Bob's,
Some to punch cattle, some to shoot,
Some for a vision, some for loot;
Some for views and some for vice,
Some for faro, some for dice;
Some for the joy for a galloping hoof,
Some for the prairie's spacious roof,
Some to forget a face, a fan,
Some to plumb the heart of man;
Some to preach and some to blow,
Some to grab and some to grow,
Some in anger, some in pride,
Some to taste, before they died,
Life served hot and a la cartee—
And some to dodge a necktie-party.

—Medora Nights

Many Chinese towns could be found on the early frontier. The men who came to work the ranches and mines and build the railroads preferred to live in their own communities. The architecture was typical of other western towns and would look more familiar to Wyatt Earp than to a resident of Canton, where many of the Chinese came from. Faced with suspicion and prejudice the Chinese turned inward and became self-sufficient. Chinese towns often boasted of their own barbers, blacksmiths, schoolteachers and doctors. These towns were viewed as places of mystery and danger by the white communities who rarely ventured into them except to find some household help.

—Stan Steiner, *Fusang: The Chinese Who Built America*

The building of the last 1900-mile link of the first transcontinental telegraph had begun back in 1844, when Samuel F. B. Morse flashed his historic first message, "What hath God wrought!" from Washington, D.C., to nearby Baltimore. During the next decade larger cities over the East were connected with telegraph lines. By 1861 one had been stretched to old Fort Kearny in central Nebraska. California too had built its telegraph lines with one reaching eastward as far as Carson City, Nevada. How to build the line over the plains, the Rockies, the Great Basin was the challenging problem....Hiram Sibley, through the Western Union, went ahead. The Pacific Telegraph Company was organized for the construction work from Omaha west to Salt Lake City. Edward Creighton was in charge of that division. Another similar company, with James Gamble as its leader, was organized to do the line-building from Carson City west to the Utah capital. In April, 1861, the race started, with an extra reward promised to the group that was first to reach Salt Lake City.

—Howard R. Driggs, *The Old West Speaks*

WESTERN UNION
TELEGRAPH COMPANY

The few decent, single women in town were widely courted. When a new school teacher arrived or when a family with one or more marriageable daughters moved into town, many an otherwise tough miner began to think of taking a bath and securing a better suit of clothes. The stricken male would spruce up his appearance—he would slick down his hair with soap, trim his beard—and he would go to church to secure an introduction to the lady of his choice. If given the encouragement of ever so fleeting a smile from the damsel, he would then invest in a suit of store clothes. And if the swain felt himself a fair hand with Mr. Colt's pistol, he might even purchase a derby hat, which to wear on Allen Street was to court a fight; someone would knock off such head-covering, and first one and then another would kick it along, soon making it not worth recovering. If the owner was a dude and took the incident good naturedly, the crowd usually would chip in to purchase him the regulation soft (cowboy) hat. If, however, he was an old hand who should have known better, then he had to be prepared to fight to defend his choice of headgear.

—Odie B. Faulk, *Tombstone, Myth and Reality*

Speak to me with your hands
   Speak to me with your eyes;
White in the reeds the swan sings
   An hour before it dies.

Speak to me with your heart
   And your simple breath;
The cactus blooms in the desert
   An hour before its death.

Over the dark water
   Flies the returning dove
Holding the morning in its beak;
   Speak to me with your love.

—John Smith, "Speak to Me With Your Hands"

There is no other beauty like Western beauty. There are no other colors like Western colors. There are no other skies with the bright, living intensity of Western skies. No other sweeping vistas anywhere else could match the magnitude of the broad avenues Nature has sculptured in the West. When God was handing out the grandeur, he planted much of it in that portion of the country.

—Olive Stokes Mix, *The Fabulous Tom Mix*

Father's regard for the land was equaled by his respect for the law and his detestation for the lawless element so prevalent in the West. I have heard him say many times that, while the law might not be entirely just, it generally expressed the will of the decent folks who were trying to build up the country, and that until someone could offer a better safeguard for a man's rights, enforcement of the law was the duty of every man who asked for its protection in any way.

My grandfather and he were in accord on that matter, as well as in the belief that the Western country could never amount to much until the lawless element had been put down. They had greater contempt for those who lacked the courage to enforce the law than for the outlaws themselves, and expressed it freely. We boys had their opinions literally drummed into us. It doesn't seem far-fetched to assume that they had lasting effect.

—Wyatt Earp

He wears a big hat and big spurs and all that,
And leggins of fancy fringed leather;
He takes pride in his boots and the pistol he shoots
And he's happy in all kinds of weather;
He's fond of his horse, it's a broncho, of course,
For oh, he can ride like the devil;
He is old for his years and he always appears
Like a fellow who's lived on the level;

He can sing, he can cook, yet his eyes have the look
Of a man that to fear is a stranger;
Yes, his cool, quiet nerve will always subserve
For his wild life of duty and danger.
He gets little to eat, and he guys tenderfeet,
And for fashion, oh well! he's not in it;
But he'll rope a gay steer when he gets on its ear
At the rate of two-forty a minute.

—Cowboy song

I'm the daddy of all the badmen that ever come from Buzzard Hole. I wuz nursed on whisky, cut my teeth on a circular saw, and rattlesnakes wuz my playmates. Us reptiles bite each other to see who's the most piz'nous, and I always win.

I'm a death-dealin' demon from Dead Man's Gulch. The further up you go, the tougher they get, and I hole up a mile past the last camp. I wuz cradled on cholla spines. Grizzlies and catamounts wuz my early playmates, and I'm so hard I kick fire outa flint with my bare toes. I have to put tarantulas and vinegaroons in my whisky to give it flavor, and mix it with strychnine and wolf pizen to give it bite. When I come to town, all the other killers hide under their mammy's aprons. Hide out little ones, it's my night to drink gore.

—Ramon F. Adams, *The Old-Time Cowhand*

Since my coming to Tombstone in 1879 the county of Cochise has been ruled by what amounts to a reign of terror. Outlaws are commonly referred to as cowboys. Not all cowboys are outlaws, but all outlaws are cowboys the way they herd stolen cattle over the desert. They ride the trails, robbing and killing travelers, robbing stages, and if they are arrested, they go free because people refuse to appear against them for fear of retaliation.

—John Montgomery, a resident of Tombstone

The situation in Tombstone was aggravated by the general feeling among the citizens that the peace officers of the county under Sheriff John Behan were in sympathy with the lawless element which roamed southeastern Arizona and it was deemed wise to guard against possible depredations of these outlaws. Our plans for law enforcement and protection of our lives and property were fully and freely discussed with Wyatt Earp and his brother Virgil. This fact establishes beyond any question the high esteem and confidence which the leading citizens of Tombstone entertained toward both Wyatt and Virgil.

—John P. Clum, editor of *The Tombstone Epitaph*

COCHISE
COUNTY

Wyatt Earp was simply not the creation known to the public through literature available today. He was a real warm-hearted, flesh-and-blood man, not gregarious but also not a cold-blooded killer as some have painted him; he was not a gunman.

—Josephine Earp

From personal experience and from numerous six-gun battles which I witnessed, I can only support the opinion advanced by the men who gave me my most valuable instruction in fast and accurate shooting, which was that the gun-fanner and the hip-shooter stood small chance to live against a man who, as old Jack Gallagher always put it, took his time and pulled the trigger once.

—Wyatt Earp

As the result of our resemblance at the time we went to Tombstone, Virg, Morg, and I were the subjects of some betting. To settle the argument, we were weighed and measured. Boots off, there wasn't a quarter-inch difference in our heights; each was just over the six-foot mark. There wasn't three pounds difference in our weights, and not one of us scaled above a hundred and fifty-eight. Virg was the heaviest, Morg a shade heavier than I. When you add that each of us had wavy, light-brown hair, blue eyes, and a mustache of the sweeping variety then in Western fashion, you may understand why our comings and goings often were reported inaccurately and why certain persons in Arizona afixed supernatural qualities to the Earps.

—Wyatt Earp

Wyatt describes the murder of Frank Stilwell:

"Stilwell caught the barrel of my Wells-Fargo gun with both hands, his left hand uppermost, almost covering the muzzles, and the right well down. I've never forgotten the look in Frank Stilwell's eyes, or the expression that came over his face as he struggled for the gun.

"I forced the gun down until the muzzle of the right barrel was just underneath Stilwell's heart. I had not spoken to him, and did not at any time. But Stilwell found his voice. You'd guess a million times wrong, without guessing what he said. I'll tell you, and you can make what you care to out of it.

"'Morg!' he said, and then a second time, 'Morg!' I've often wondered what made him say that."

"What happened then?" (Stuart Lake, biographer)

"I let him have it."

—Stuart Lake, *Wyatt Earp, Frontier Marshal*

DRAIN DAIL

58

Singing through the forests,
Rattling over ridges,
Shooting under arches,
Rumbing over bridges,
Whizzing through the mountains,
Buzzing o'er the vale.
Bless me! This is pleasant,
Riding on the rail !

—John Godfrey Saxe

Doc arrived in Ft. Griffin, Texas, where he made the acquaintance of Kate Fisher (also referred to as Elder), better known around Ft. Griffin as Big Nose Kate. This acquaintance ripened into sincere friendship and upon state occasions, Doc would introduce her as Mrs. Doc Holliday. It was in Ft. Griffin that Doc also made the acquaintance of Wyatt Earp who was on the trail of a group of cattle thieves.

—Published by the *San Francisco Weekly Examiner*, August 6, 1896,
based on information supplied by Wyatt Earp

The young fellow who came into the office was so slim as to give a mistaken impression of his height, and was unusually pallid for the plains country. He was about five feet ten inches tall, but couldn't have weighed more than one hundred and thirty pounds. If his face had not been emaciated, he might have been handsome; he looked to be a man of intelligence and good breeding. From the moment I laid eyes on him, Doc Holliday's appearance haunted me—it does to this day—with his large blue eyes set deep in a haggard face, his heavy head of wavy, ash-blond hair, and his neatly trimmed mustache, his really fine nose and his very expressive mouth.

—Wyatt Earp

The gambler, from about 1850 to 1880, was among the aristocrats of western society. Many came from Mississippi steamboats, from Natchez Plantations and from Chicago's sand district. They all considered themselves gentlemen, were often womanizers and flashy dressers, sporting black suits with frilled snowy shirts and brocaded vests. Snobbery existed within the fraternity. It was principally the faro dealers, and to a lesser extent the holders of lansquenet and Spanish monte banks, who made up the flashily dressed upper stratum of gambling society. Why this was so is hard to say. . . .

Unlike the amateur gambler who could take his losses in stride, the pro had to win more often than he lost or he did not eat. Not all amateurs showed the required equanimity when losing heavily. They were apt to seize the dealer by the throat, sticking a pistol in his face while going for the pot. Their excuse, was, of course, that the dealer had cheated. Probably he had. In order to live, he had to win. If he wanted to win, he had to give Dame Fortune a helping hand. The dexterous gent was admired. It was only the clumsy tinhorn who tried to deal from the bottom who was despised.

A common affliction among gamblers was tuberculosis, which was often aggravated by days and nights in dark, smoke-filled rooms, forty-eight hour card games and a diet of black coffee, whiskey and cheroots. This often gave the professional gambler the edge in a showdown. He knew he was going to die sooner or later, so what if it was sooner?

Although many of the gamblers won hundreds of thousands of dollars during a lifetime, most of them died broke. When coming to the end of the road gamblers invariably blew their brains out with a derringer. Lady gamblers, however, often swallowed poison or jumped into the river in order to look pretty and undisfigured even in death.

—Richard Erdoes, *Saloons of the Old West*

The most famous of the "lady gams," as they were known, was Eleanor Dumont, also known as Madame Mustache. She was French born and knew how to defend herself with horsewhip or pistol if the situation demanded it. She opened an elegant gambling saloon in 1850 in Nevada City, offering free champagne in unlimited quantities to all her customers. She shifted her operations from camp to camp, following the gold and silver strikes, finally ending up in Bodie, where she lost what little money she had left at faro and ended her career by mixing up a cocktail of half champagne and half prussic acid.

—Richard Erdoes, *Saloons of the Old West*

What Things Cost

- A "good" meal is fifty cents.
- A hundred pounds of flour is $6.
- A pound of potatoes is four cents.
- A pound of bacon is twenty cents.
- A pound of ham is 16 to 20 cents.
- A pound of steak is eight to fifteen cents.
- A gallon of whiskey is $2 to $8.
- A gallon of mescal is $4.
- A dozen home-made beers are $3.
- A dozen imported beers are $5. (Coors would be imported from Colorado)
- A gallon of turpentine is $2.
- A steel hammer is 35 to 50 cents.
- A keg of nails is $14.
- A keg of horse shoes is $14.
- A dozen axes are $15 to $24.
- A good wool mattress is $6.
- A pillow costs $1.
- A wooden chair costs $1.
- A plain table costs $6.
- A lamp costs $6.
- A curtain costs $1.25.
- A pen rack costs $1.
- A journal and ledger costs $2.
- A basin and glass costs $1.
- A shanty that cost $50 to build rents for $15 a month.
- A lot 30 by 80 feet, on Allen Street, between Fourth and Sixth, is worth $6,000.
- A dozen eggs cost seventy-five cents.
- A yard of calico costs twenty-five cents.
- A pair of dusters can be had "on sale" at the San Jose House for twenty-five cents.

—Bob Boze Bell, *The Illustrated Life & Times of Wyatt Earp*

LEONARD & YOUNG
GENERAL
MERCHANDISE

The Tombstone Stagecoach:

John Pleasant Gray, a Californian who came to Tombstone in 1880, described his journey on the Tucson and Tombstone Express: That day's stage ride will always live in my memory—but not for its beauty spots. Jammed like sardines on the hard seats of an old time leather spring coach—a Concord—leaving Pantano, creeping much of the way, letting the horses walk, through miles of alkali dust that the wheels rolled up in thick clouds of which we received the full benefit, we couldn't then see much romance in the old stage method of travelling...If it had not been for the long stretches when the horses had to walk, enabling most of us to get out and "foot it" as a relaxation, it seems as if we could never have survived the trip.

—Odie B. Faulk, *Tombstone, Myth and Reality*

The sunlight clasps the earth
  And the moonbeams kiss the sea:
What is all this sweet work worth
If thou kiss not me?
—Percy Bysshe Shelley, "Love's Philosophy"

Josephine Sarah Marcus moved with her parents and two sisters, Edna and Henrietta, from Brooklyn to San Francisco in the late 1860s. In 1879, when Josie was eighteen, the *H.M.S. Pinafore* craze swept the country. Josie claims that her best friend, Dora, persuaded her to run away from home and join the Pauline Markham Troupe which was traveling the country with a production of the popular show. The company crossed the southwest by stage, playing in Los Angeles, San Bernadino, Prescott, Arizona, and finally Tombstone. On the way to Prescott a raid by Apaches was warded off by a string of riders led by Johnny Behan, who was, to her young eyes, a dashing, romantic rescuer. The much older Johnny took an interest in the young actress, proposed marriage and asked her to join him in the new boom camp of Tombstone. She left to join her fiance in Tombstone where she got her first glimpse of an Earp, Morgan, who was the shotgun messenger on her stage. Upon arrival she caught a quick glimpse of Wyatt before Johnny whisked her away to show her off around town.

—*I Married Wyatt Earp: The Recollections of Josephine Sarah Marcus Earp,*
collected and edited by Glenn G. Boyer

As chief of police of Tombstone, Virgil helped a lot of trouble simply to melt away because of his calm, imperturbable nature. Many officers nervously cause more trouble than they can handle. That wasn't Virge. In addition, on a frontier which was notorious for fast and loose operators on the small-town police forces, Virgil was scrupulously honest. I recall Wyatt telling me of one night in Tombstone when Virgil relieved a falling-down drunk visitor of a thousand-dollar bank roll for safe keeping till he sobered up in the morning. Some of the town sharpies had had their eyes on the man when Virgil took him in tow. This fortunate fellow apparently couldn't believe it when Virge returned his money and refused a reward.

—Josie Earp

REWARD!
$800
$300.00

A&P RR. CO.
107
CONTENTION

Oh, a man there lives on the Western plains,
With a ton of fight and an ounce of brains
Who herds the cows as he robs the trains
And goes by the name of cowboy.
He laughs at death and scoffs at life;
He feels unwell unless in some strife.
He fights with a pistol, a rifle, or knife,
This reckless, rollicking cowboy.

He shoots out lights in a dancing hall;
He gets shot up in a drunken brawl.
Some coroner's jury then ends it all,
And that's the last of the cowboy.

—Richard Erdoes, *Saloons Of the Old West*

JUSTICE
LAW and
Order

MURDER
MURDER

Whatever else may be said of Wyatt Earp, against or for him, and no matter what his motives, the greatest gun-fighter that the Old West knew cleaned up Tombstone, the toughest camp in the world.

—Stuart Lake, *Wyatt Earp, Frontier Marshal*

GENERAL
MERCHANDISE

The profoundest of all sensualities
is the sense of truth
and the next deepest sensual experience
is the sense of justice.

—D. H. Lawrence, "The Deepest Sensuality"

PHOTOGRAPHY
STUDIO

For my handling of the situation at Tombstone, I have no regrets. Were it to be done over again, I would do exactly as I did at that time. If the outlaws and their friends and allies imagined that they could intimidate or exterminate the Earps by a process of assassination, and then hide behind alibis and the technicalities of the law, they simply missed their guess.

—Wyatt Earp

Truth doesn't matter so much, so long as it lives.

—Jack London

Production

Wyatt Earp began filming Monday, July 19, 1993, in Sante Fe, New Mexico. Five months later, on December 14, we shot the final image onboard *The Spirit of '98* at the base of the Olympic Mountain Range outside Port Angeles, Washington. We employed over a thousand persons, expending half a million man-hours, and catered 27,000 meals. Complete Western towns were designed, built, and dismantled. We put over 125 miles of film through our numerous cameras, and spent tens of millions of dollars, in the hopes of creating a beautiful film that entertains the world for future generations to come.

—Jim Wilson

Wyatt Earp's West Photographs

Listings indicate the photograph's subject, filming location, and technical specifications. All photographs were taken by a Nikon F4 unless otherwise stated.

p. i. Wyatt Earp (Kevin Costner) near the OK Corral. Cook Ranch, Galisteo, NM. Photographed from a roof top using an 85mm Nikkor lens at an exposure of 1/125 at f8 on Ektachrome Lumiere 100X film.

p. ii. Wyatt Earp and Sallie (Tea Leoni) watch the fireworks outside of Lucky's Saloon, Wyoming. Cook Ranch, Galisteo, NM. 24mm Nikkor lens at an exposure of 1/30 at f4 on Ektachrome 320T film.

p. viii. Kevin Costner with safety face-shield prepares to fire on Frank Stillwell as loader Eric Roizman slates B Camera in trainyard, Tucson, AZ. The Cumbres and Toltec Scenic Railroad, Chama, NM. AF-Nikkor 20mm lens at an exposure of 1/60 at f5.6 on Tmax p3200 film.

p. 3. Highway man (Billy Burton, Jr.) rears his horse as he loses pursuit of Wyatt and Dutch's fleeing wagon on a canyon road, in Wyoming. Cook Ranch, Galisteo, NM. Photographed while hiding under a bush using a 20mm Nikkor lens at an exposure of 1/250 at f8 on Tmax 400 film.

pp. 4-5. The Earp family wagon travels west. Ghost Ranch, NM. 105mm Nikkor lens at an exposure of 1/125 at f16 on Kodachrome 64 film.

p. 7. Virginia Earp (Betty Buckley) and child wait out a dust storm with James Earp (David Andrews) and the family dog, Sage, in the Mojave desert. Zia Pueblo, NM. 24mm Nikkor lens with an 81A filter at an exposure of 1/60 at f5.6 on Ektachrome 100 Plus film.

pp. 8-9. Nicholas Earp (Gene Hackman) and young Warren (Oliver Hendrickson) lead the Earp family wagon-train to Omaha, Nebraska, with Virgina Earp (Betty Buckley) and young Wyatt (Ian Bohen) following behind. Ghost Ranch, NM. 50mm Nikkor lens with an 81A filter, at an exposure of 1/250 at f8 on Kodachrome 200 film.

p. 10 Young Wyatt (Ian Bohen) stands in a dust storm in the Mojave Desert. Zia Pueblo, NM. 105mm Nikkor lens at an exposure of 1/250 at f5.6 on Tmax 400 film.

p. 11. Young Wyatt (Ian Bohen) runs off through a cornfield in Pella, IA, to join the Civil War. King Ranch, Stanley, NM. Photographed from a crane with a 35mm Nikkor lens with a yellow Wratten No. 8 filter at an exposure of 1/125 at f8 on Tmax 400 film.

pp. 12-13. Wyatt Earp drives a team of horses through a canyon road in Wyoming as Dutch Wiley (Monty Stuart) fires on the pursuing highway men. Cook Ranch, Galisteo, NM. Photographed from a speeding camera car using a 28mm Nikkor lens with a yellow Wratten No. 8 filter at an exposure of 1/500 at f5.6 on Tmax 400 film.

pp. 14-15. Wyatt Earp and Dutch Wiley (Monty Stuart) race their wagon through a canyon in Wyoming, fleeing from highway men. Cook Ranch, Galisteo, NM. Photographed from a canyon ridge using an AF-Nikkor 35-135mm lens at an exposure of 1/250 at f5.6 on Kodachrome 200 film.

p. 16. Wyatt Earp rides into Fort Griffin with a captured Dave Rudabaugh. Eaves Ranch, NM. Photographed from a top of a windmill using a 50mm Nikkor lens with an 81B filter at an exposure of 1/250 at f5.6 on Kodachrome 200 film.

p. 17. Wranglers hold cattle at the Wichita Stockyard. Cook Ranch, Galisteo, NM. 35mm Nikkor lens with an 81B filter at an exposure of 1/125 at f5.6 on Kodachrome 200 film.

pp. 18-19. Townspeople on the main streeet of Omaha, NE. Eaves Ranch, Sante Fe, NM. Photographed from a crane with a 35mm Nikkor lens at an exposure of 1/250 at f5.6 on Ektachrome Lumiere 100X film.

p 20. John Shanssey (Michael McGrady) takes a punch as Mike Donovan (Clark Sanchez) follows through with right hook in a Wyoming rail camp's boxing ring. Cook Ranch, Galisteo, NM. AF-Nikkor 20mm lens at an exposure of 1/500 at f5.6 on Tmax 400 film.

p. 21. Wyatt Earp referees a boxing match between Shanssey and Donovan on the morning of the Fourth of July in a Wyoming railway camp. Cook Ranch, Galisteo, NM. 24mm Nikkor lens at an exposure of 1/250 at f8 on Ektachrome Lumiere 100X film.

pp. 22-23. The Clanton gang, (l to r) Billy Claiboure (Chris Kamm), Frank McLaury (Rex Linn), Curly Bill (Lewis Smith), Frank Stillwell (John Dennis Johnston), Ike Clanton (Jeff Fahey), Johnny Ringo (Norman Howell), Indian Charlie (Scotty Augare), Pete Spence (Kirk Fox), Tom McLaury (Adam Baldwin), and Billy Clanton (Gabriel Golsey). Cook Ranch, Galisteo, NM. 24mm Nikkor lens at an exposure of 1/60 at f8 on Ektachrome 100 Plus film.

p. 24. Railway workers pound stakes and dig trenches for new rails on the Great Plains of Wyoming. Cook Ranch, Galisteo, NM. 80-200mm Nikkor lens at an exposure of 1/250 at f5.6 on Ektachrome 100 Plus film.

p. 25. Chinatown, Tombstone, AZ. Cook Ranch, Galisteo, NM. 50mm Nikkor lens with an Enhancing filter at an exposure of 1/125 at f5.6 on Ektachrome Lumiere 100X film.

p. 26. Wyatt Earp in the Western Union office, Fort Griffin. Eaves Ranch, Sante Fe, NM. Photographed through the window using an AF-Nikkor 80-200mm lens at an exposure of 1/250 at f5.6 on Tmax 400 film.

p. 27. Wyatt Earp reads the news of Ed Masterson's murder in the Western Union office, Fort Griffin. Eaves Ranch, Sante Fe, NM. AF-Nikkor 180 mm lens at an exposure of 1/250 at f5.6 on Tmax 400 film.

p. 28. Wyatt Earp readies himself to visit Urilla Sutherland (Annabeth Gish) in Lamar, Missouri. Las Vegas, NM. AF-Nikkor 80-200mm lens at an exposure of 1/250 at f4 on Ektachrome 100 Plus film.

p. 29. Judge Earp (Giorgio Taipale) marries Wyatt Earp to Urilla Sutherland (Annabeth Gish) with the Earp and Sutherland families in attendance on a hilltop on the edge of Lamar, Missouri. Los Golondrinas, NM. 200mm Nikkor lens at an exposure of 1/125 at f5.6 on Ektachrome 100 Plus film.

p. 30. Young boys watch Wyatt Earp ride into Fort Griffin with Dave Rudabaugh. Eaves Ranch, Sante Fe, NM. 135mm Nikkor lens with an 81A filter at an exposure of 1/250 at f5.6 on Kodachrome 200 film.

p. 31. Young girls (l. to r.: Deja Mae Howell, Lauren Wilson, and Amanda Grillo) hide muffins at the Earp wedding. Los Golondrinos, NM. 24mm Nikkor lens at an exposure of 1/60 at f5.6 on Ektachrome 100 Plus film.

pp. 32-33. Virgil Earp (Michael Madsen) looks back at Allie (Catherine O'Hara) the morning of the shoot-out at the OK Corral. Cook Ranch, Galisteo, NM. 35mm Nikkor lens at an exposure of 1/60 at f8 on Ektachrome Lumiere 100X film

p. 34. Tent Rocks, Cochiti Pueblo, NM. ELK Hasselblad using a 40mm Distagon lens with an 81B glass filter at an exposure of 1/125 at f8 on Ektachrome 100 Plus film.

p. 35. Aspen trees, Sangre de Cristol Mountains, NM: 105mm Nikkor lens with an Enhancing filter at an exposure of 1/125 at f5.6 on Ektachrome Lumiere 100X.

p. 36. Horses drinking in the Pecos River, NM. 200mm Nikkor lens at an exposure of 1/250 at f5.6 on Kodachrome 200 film.

p. 37. Rainbow after a late afternoon rainfall, Cook Ranch, Galisteo, NM. 35mm Nikkor lens with a polarizing filter, at an exposure of 1/60 at f5.6 on Kodachrome 200 film.

p. 38. Morgan Earp (Linden Ashby), Wyatt Earp, and Marshall White (Boots Sutherland) ride into Tombstone with Frank Stillwell (John Dennis Johnston). Cook Ranch, Galisteo, NM. 80-200mm Nikkor lens with an 81A filter at an exposure of 1/250 at f8 on Kodachrome 200 film.

p. 39. Nicholas Earp (Gene Hackman) searches for young Wyatt in a cornfield in Pella, Iowa. King Ranch, Stanley, NM. 105mm Nikkor lens at an exposure of 1/125 at f5.6 on Ektachrome 100 Plus film.

p. 40. Doc Holliday (Dennis Quaid) turns his horse around to go after Johnny Ringo at Mescal Spring in the Whetstone Mountains. Plaza Blanca Pueblo, NM. 135mm Nikkor lens at an exposure of 1/250 at f5.6 on Tmax 400 film.

p. 41 Young Wyatt Earp (Ian Logan) takes a fall after horse steps in a varmint hole. Ghost Ranch, NM. AF-Nikkor 35-135mm lens at an exposure of 1/250 at f5.6 on Ektachrome 100 Plus film.

p. 42. Turkey Creek Jack (head wrangler Rusty Henrickson), takes a stunt fall during the Mescal Spring shoot-out. Whetstone Mountains, NM. 35mm Nikkor lens with a red Wratten No. 23A filter, at an exposure of 1/500 at f5.6 on Tmax p3200 film.

p. 43. Highway stuntman Shawn Howell takes a dive after flipping his horse during the pursuit of Wyatt and Dutch, Wyoming. Photographed under A camera with a 24mm Nikkor lens using a red Wratten 25 filter at an exposure of 1/250 at f8 on Tmax 3200 film.

p. 44. Stuntman Benny Manning flies through a window of the Comique Theatre and Saloon, Dodge City, after being shot by Ed Masterton. Cook Ranch, Galisteo, NM. 50mm Nikkor lens at an exposure of 1/500 at f1.2 on Ektachrome 320T film.

p. 45. Morgan Earp (Linden Ashby) lies dead in Hatch's Saloon, Tombstone, Doctor Goodfellow (producer Jim Wilson) and Wyatt Earp look on as Lou Earp (Alison Elliott) grieves. Cook Ranch, Galisteo, NM. 35mm Nikkor lens with an exposure of 1/60 at f4 on Ektachrome 320T film.

p. 46. Sheriff Behan (Mark Harmon) in the Oriental Saloon. Cook Ranch, Galisteo, NM. Photographed using an ELX Hasselblad with a 150mm Sonnar lens using an 81A gel filter at an exposure of 1/125 at f8 on Ektachrome Lumiere 100X film.

p. 47. Sheriff Behan (Mark Harmon, center) and Ike Clanton (Jeff Fahey, right) in front of the Tombstone Court House mount up the posse to pursue Wyatt Earp and his men. Cook Ranch, Galisteo, NM. Photographed using an ELX Hasselblad with a 40mm Distagon lens using an 81B glass filter at an exposure of 1/125 at f8 on Ektachrome Lumiere 100X film.

p. 48. Wyatt Earp. Cook Ranch, Galisteo, NM. Photographed using an ELX Hasselblad with a 80mm Planar lens, with an 81B gel filter at an exposure of 1/125 at f8 on Ektachrome 100X film.

p. 49. Wyatt Earp. Plaza Blanca Pueblo, NM. AF-20mm Nikkor lens with a polarizing filter at an exposure of 1/60 at f8 on Kodachrome 200 film.

p. 50. Wyatt Earp. Plaza Blanca Pueblo, NM. Photographed after Kevin spots me hiding in the rocks using an AF Nikkor 80-200mm lens with an exposure of 1/250 at f5.6 on Tmax 400 film.

p. 51. Wyatt Earp blasts Curly Bill (Lewis Smith) dead in Mescal Spring. Plaza Blanca Pueblo, NM. 35mm Nikkor lens with a yellow Wratten No. 8 filter at an exposure of 1/125 at f8 on Tmax 400 film.

p. 52. The Earp Family in Tombstone: (l. to r., back row): Virgil (Michael Madsen), Wyatt, Morgan (Linden Ashby), and James (David Andrews) (l.to r, bottom row): Allie (Catherine O'Hara), Mattie (Mare Winningham), Lou (Alison Elliott), and Bessie (Jobeth Williams). Cook Ranch, Galisteo, NM. 35mm Nikkor lens with an exposure of 1/125 at f5.6 on Ektachrome 100 Plus film.

p. 53. Nicholas Earp (Gene Hackman, center) talks about family values and going to California with his children in the Earp Farmhouse, Iowa. Garson Studios, Sante Fe, NM. 50mm Nikkor lens at an exposure of 1/60 at f4 on Ektachrome 320T film.

p. 54. Doc Holliday (Dennis Quaid, right) stops Wyatt Earp from the continuous shooting of Frank Stillwell in the Tucson trainyard. The Cumbres and Toltec Scenic Railroad, Chama, NM. 35mm Nikkor lens at an exposure of 1/30 at f2 on Ektachrome 400 film.

p. 55. Wyatt Earp prepares to blast Frank Stillwell (John Dennis Johnston, right) in the Tucson railyard. The Cumbres and Toltec Scenic Railroad, Chama, NM. 24mm Nikkor lens at an exposure of 1/60 at f4 on Ektachrome 400 film.

p. 56. Wyatt Earp prepares to shoot in the Tucson railyard. The Cumbres and Toltec Scenic Railroad, Chama, NM. 35mm Nikkor lens with an exposure of 1/60 at f1.4 on Ektachrome 400 film.

p. 57. Passengers depart train in Tucson railyard. The Cumbres and Toltec Scenic Railroad, Chama, NM. 50mm Nikkor lens with an exposure of 1/60 at f4 on Ektachrome 400 film.

p. 58. Train at sunset in Contention, AZ. Antonito, CO. 105mm Nikkor lens with an exposure of 1/125 at f1.8 on Kodachrome 200 film.

p. 59. Train prepares to depart at sunset from depot in Contention, AZ. Antonito, CO. 28mm Nikkor lens with an exposure of 1/30 at f5.6 on Kodachrome 200 film.

pp. 60-61. Train waits at depot at Contention, AZ. Antonito, CO. 24mm Nikkor lens with a polarizing filter with at an exposure of 1/125 at f5.6 on Ektachrome Lumiere 100X film.

p. 62. Doc Holliday (Dennis Quaid) and Big Nose Kate (Isabella Rossellini) in the Oriental Saloon. Cook Ranch, Galisteo, NM. ELX Hasselblad with an 80mm Planar lens, using an 81A gel filter, with an exposure of 1/125 at f8 on Ektachrome Lumiere 100X film.

p. 63. Doc Holliday (Dennis Quaid) in the Tombstone jail. Big Nose Kate (Isabella Rossellini) in the Oriental Saloon. Cook Ranch, Galisteo, NM. ELX Hasselbld with a 150mm Sonnar lens, using an 81A gel filter at an exposure of 1/125 at f8 on Ektachrome Lumiere 100X film.

p. 64. Doc Holliday (Dennis Quaid, right) talks with Wyatt about Mr. Death in the Oriental Saloon, Tombstone. Cook Ranch, Galisteo, NM. 50mm Nikkor lens with an exposure of 1/60 at f2.8 on Ektachrome 320T film.

p. 65. Doc Holiday (Dennis Quaid) prepares to shoot Johnny Ringo at Mescal Spring, Whetstone Mountains. Plaza Blanca Pueblo, NM. 35mm Nikkor lens with an 81A filter, at an exposure of 1/125 at f4 on Ektachrome 100 film.

p. 67. James Earp (David Andrews, left) gambles with Doc Holliday in the Oriental Saloon, Tombstone. Cook Ranch, Galisteo, NM. 105mm Nikkor lens with an exposure of 1/60 at f4 on Ektachrome 320T film.

p. 68. Buffalo barmaid (costumer Ruby Manis) flirts with a hidesman in the Tent Saloon, Buffalo Camp, Kansas plains. Garson Studios, Sante Fe, NM. 105mm Nikkor lens with an exposure of 1/125 at f4 on Ektachrome 320T film.

p. 69. Wyatt Earp watches Doc Holliday and Big Nose Kate play poker with gambler Homer (director Larry Kasdan, far right) at the Oriental Saloon, Tombstone. Cook Ranch, Galisteo, NM. 35 mm Nikkor lens with an exposure of 1/60 at f5.6 on Ektachrome 320T film.

p. 70. A chandelier crashes into a table at the Comique Theatre, Dodge City, as stuntwoman Beau Holden (left), Tricia Howell (center), and Mark Thomason scramble. Doc Holliday (Dennis Quaid, far right) continues to play cards. Cook Ranch, Galisteo, NM. 24mm Nikkor lens with an exposure of 1/250 at f5.6 on Tmax p3200 film.

p. 71. A drunken Wyatt sits in a tub while Paris (Ellen Blake), a whore in a Pine Bluff, Arkansas, brothel pours him a drink. Cook Ranch, Galisteo, NM. 50mm Nikkor lens with an exposure of 1/60 at f4 on Ektachrome 320T film.

p. 72. James Earp (David Andrews) pitches cards in Hatch's Saloon. Cook Ranch, Galisteo, NM. photographed with an ELX Hasselblad with an 80mm Planar lens with an 81A gel filter, at an exposure of f5.6 on Ektachrome Lumiere 100X film.

p. 73. Bartender (John Furlong) at the Oriental Saloon, Tombstone. Cook Ranch, Galisteo, NM. photographed with an ELX Hasselblad with an 80mm Planar lens at an exposure of 1/125 at f5.6 on Ektachrome Lumiere 100X film.

p. 74. Town extra sleeping with dog. Cook Ranch, Galisteo, NM. 135mm Nikkor lens with an exposure of 1/125 at f8 on Tmax 400 film.

p. 76. General store, Tombstone. Cook Ranch, Galisteo, NM. 28mm Nikkor lens with an 81C filter, at an exposure of 1/125 at f8 on Ektachrome Lumiere 100X film.

p. 77. Pigs at the Earp family farmhouse, Iowa. King Ranch, Stanley, NM. 24mm Nikkor lens with an 81B filter at an exposure of 1/125 at f11 on Kodachrome 200 film.

p. 78. Josie (Joanna Going) sees Wyatt Earp on her arrival in Tombstone. Cook Ranch, Galisteo, NM. 200mm Nikkor lens with an 81A filter with an exposure of 1/250 at f5.6 on Kodachrome 200 film.

p. 79. Sheriff Behan (Mark Harmon) kisses Josie (Joanna Going) in front of the Tombstone stage coach. Cook Ranch, Galisteo, NM. AF-Nikkor 35-135mm lens with an 81A filter with an exposure of 1/125 at f8 on Kodachrome 200 film.

p. 80. Josie (Joanna Going) and Wyatt Earp in Josie's bungalow, Tombstone. Cook Ranch, Galisteo, NM. 24mm Nikkor lens at an exposure of 1/30 at f2 on Ektachrome 320T film.

p. 81. Wyatt tells Josie (Joanna Going) goodbye in Josie's room at the Cosmopolitan Hotel. Garson Studios, Sante Fe, NM. 105mm Nikkor lens with an exposure of 1/125 at f8 on Ektachrome 320T film.

p. 81. Wyatt and Josie (Joanna Going) on the deck of a steamship off the coast of Alaska. Wyatt points to their gold in the mountains. Port Angeles, WA. 35mm Nikkor lens with an exposure of 1/125 at f5.6 on Ektachrome 100 Plus film.

pp. 82-83. Wyatt and Josie (Joanna Going) stand in a meadow. Black Mesa Mountain by the Rio Grande River, NM. 85mm Nikkor lens with an 81C filter at an exposure of 1/125 at f8 on Ektachrome Lumiere 100X film.

p. 84. Josie (Joanna Going) stops to talk with Wyatt on a boardwalk of Tombstone. Cook Ranch, Galisteo, NM. 135mm Nikkor lens with an Enhancing filter, at an exposure of 1/125 at f4 on Ektachrome 100 Lumiere 100X film.

p. 85. Josie (Joanna Going) in the Oriental Saloon. Cook Ranch, Galisteo, NM. ELX Hasselblad with 150mm Distagon lens, at an exposure of 1/125 at f8 on Tmax 100 film.

p. 86. Ed Masterton (Bill Pullman, foreground) shoots at Wagner (Dick Beach) in the Comique Theatre and Saloon. Cook Ranch, Galisteo, NM. 24mm Nikkor lens with an exposure of 1/125 at f5.6 on Tmax p3200 film.

p. 87. Virgil Earp (Michael Madsen) in the Tombstone jail. Cook Ranch, Galisteo, NM. ELX Hasselblad with an 80mm Planar lens with an 81A gel filter, with an exposure of 1/125 at f11 on Ektachrome Lumiere 100X film.

p. 88. Wyatt, Warren Earp (James Caviezel, right), and Sherman McMsters (Todd Allen) load Morgan's casket onto the train at the Contention, AZ, train depot. Antonito, CO. 35mm Nikkor lens with an exposure of 1/125 at f8 on Ektachrome 100 Plus film.

p. 89. Tom McLaury (Adam Baldwin), Frank McLaury (Rex Linn), and Billy Clanton (Gabriel Folse) lay dead in the front window of Ritter & Ream City Undertakers, as an on-looker passes by. Cook Ranch, Galisteo, NM. 35mm Nikkor lens with an exposure of 1/125 at f5.6 on Ektachrome 100 Plus film.

pp. 90-91. The funeral procession for the McLaurys and Billy Clanton led by drummer (sound mixer John Pritchett, right) on Allen Street, Tombstone,. Cook Ranch, Galisteo, NM. 105mm Nikkor lens with an 81C filter, with an exposure of 1/250 at f11 on Kodachrome 200 film.

p. 93. Doc Holliday (Dennis Quaid), Morgan Earp (Linden Ashby), Wyatt Earp, and Virgil Earp (Michael Madsen) walk down Fourth Street to the OK Corral showdown. Cook Ranch, Galisteo, NM. AF-Nikkor 80-200mm lens with an 81A filter, with an exposure of 1/250 at f5.6 on Ektachrome Lumiere 100X film.

pp.. 94-95. Doc (Dennis Quaid), Morgan (Linden Ashby), Wyatt, and Virgil (Michael Madsen) pause for a moment at Fourth and Freemont Street for the final walk to the OK Corral. Cook Ranch, Galisteo, NM. 24mm Nikkor lens with an 81C filter, with an exposure of 1/250 at f11 on Kodachrome 200 film.

p. 96. Virgil (Michael Madsen), Wyatt, Morgan (Linden Ashby), and Doc (Dennis Quaid) walk up Front Street toward Freemont Street. Cook Ranch, Galisteo, NM. photographed from a rooftop ledge. AF-Nikkor 35-135mm lens with an 81C filter, with an exposure of 1/250 at f11 on Kodachrome 200 film.

p. 97. (Top to bottom) Wyatt, Morgan (Linden Ashby), and Virgil (Michael Madsen) wait at Freemont Street. Cook Ranch, Galisteo, NM. AF-Nikkor 35-135mm lens with an 81C filter, with an exposure of 1/125 at f22 on Kodachrome 200 film.

p. 98. Top photo: Tom McLaury (Adam Baldwin) aims at Morgan Earp (Linden Ashby) as Morgan fires on Frank McLaury (Rex Linn). Bottom photo: Morgan Earp takes a shoulder bullet hit from Tom McLaury's gun. Squib can be seen exploding from Morgan's shoulder. Cook Ranch, Galisteo, NM. Both were taken with a motor drive at 5.7 frames per second with a 105mm Nikkor lens with an 81C filter, with an exposure of 1/250 at f11 on Kodachrome 200 film.

Morgan's casket onto the train at the Contention, AZ, train depot. Antonito, CO. 35mm Nikkor lens with an exposure of 1/125 at f8 on Ektachrome 100 Plus film.

p. 89. Tom McLaury (Adam Baldwin), Frank McLaury (Rex Linn), and Billy Clanton (Gabriel Folse) lay dead in the front window of Ritter & Ream City Undertakers, as an on-looker passes by. Cook Ranch, Galisteo, NM. 35mm Nikkor lens with an exposure of 1/125 at f5.6 on Ektachrome 100 Plus film.

pp. 90-91. The funeral procession for the McLaurys and Billy Clanton led by drummer (sound mixer John Pritchett, right) on Allen Street, Tombstone,. Cook Ranch, Galisteo, NM. 105mm Nikkor lens with an 81C filter, with an exposure of 1/250 at f11 on Kodachrome 200 film.

p. 93. Doc Holliday (Dennis Quaid), Morgan Earp (Linden Ashby), Wyatt Earp, and Virgil Earp (Michael Madsen) walk down Fourth Street to the OK Corral showdown. Cook Ranch, Galisteo, NM. AF-Nikkor 80-200mm lens with an 81A filter, with an exposure of 1/250 at f5.6 on Ektachrome Lumiere 100X film.

pp.. 94-95. Doc (Dennis Quaid), Morgan (Linden Ashby), Wyatt, and Virgil (Michael Madsen) pause for a moment at Fourth and Freemont Street for the final walk to the OK Corral. Cook Ranch, Galisteo, NM. 24mm Nikkor lens with an 81C filter, with an exposure of 1/250 at f11 on Kodachrome 200 film.

p. 96. Virgil (Michael Madsen), Wyatt, Morgan (Linden Ashby), and Doc (Dennis Quaid) walk up Front Street toward Freemont Street. Cook Ranch, Galisteo, NM. photographed from a rooftop ledge. AF-Nikkor 35-135mm lens with an 81C filter, with an exposure of 1/250 at f11 on Kodachrome 200 film.

p. 97. (Top to bottom) Wyatt, Morgan (Linden Ashby), and Virgil (Michael Madsen) wait at Freemont Street. Cook Ranch, Galisteo, NM. AF-Nikkor 35-135mm lens with an 81C filter, with an exposure of 1/125 at f22 on Kodachrome 200 film.

p. 98. Top photo: Tom McLaury (Adam Baldwin) aims at Morgan Earp (Linden Ashby) as Morgan fires on Frank McLaury (Rex Linn). Bottom photo: Morgan Earp takes a shoulder bullet hit from Tom McLaury's gun. Squib can be seen exploding from Morgan's shoulder. Cook Ranch, Galisteo, NM. Both were taken with a motor drive at 5.7 frames per second with a 105mm Nikkor lens with an 81C filter, with an exposure of 1/250 at f11 on Kodachrome 200 film.

p. 99. Doc Holliday (Dennis Quaid, left) recoils back after blasting Tom McLaury (Adam Baldwin, right) in a vacant lot by the OK Corral. Cook Ranch, Galisteo, NM. Photographed with a motor drive at 5.7 frames per second, with a 35mm Nikkor lens with an 81C filter at 1/250 at f11 on Kodachrome 200 film.

p. 100. Tom McLaury (Adam Baldwin) falls dead in the center of Freemont Street, Tombstone, as Morgan Earp (Linden Ashby) squirms in pain on the ground. Wyatt Earp looks on. Cook Ranch, Galisteo, NM. 20mm Nikkor lens with an Enhancing filter, with an exposure of 1/250 at f8 on Ektachrome Lumiere 100X film.

p. 101. Virgil Earp (Michael Madsen) takes a moment between shooting in a vacant lot next to the OK Corral, Tombstone. Cook Ranch, Galisteo, NM. 200mm Nikkor lens with an 81A filter, with an exposure of 1/250 at f5.6 on Ektachrome 100 Plus film.

p. 102. Virgil Earp (Michel Madsen) leaves home the morning of the OK Corral showdown. Cook Ranch, Galisteo, NM. 105mm Nikkor lens with an exposure of 1/125 at f1.8 on Ektachrome Lumiere 100X film.

p. 103. Sunset at the Cook Ranch, Galisteo, NM. 135mm Nikkor lens with an exposure of 1/125 at f2 on Ektachrome Lumiere 100X film.

p. 104. Operator Bill Rose sits behind A Camera and lines up a shot. Big Nose Kate (Isabella

Acknowledgments

We gratefully acknowledge permission to reprint copyrighted material from the following sources. Numbers refer to pages in this book where text excerpts appear:

From *The Fabulous Tom Mix* © 1957 by Olive Stokes Mix. Reprinted by permission of the author: 35.

From *Forty Years on the Wild Frontier* © 1985 by Carl Breihan and Wayne Montgomery. Reprinted by permission of Devin-Adair Publishers: 45.

From *Fusang: The Chinese Who Built America* © 1979 by Stan Steiner. Reprinted by permission of HarperCollins Publishers: 25.

From *Ghost Town* © 1941 by G. Ezra Dane in collaboration with Beatrice J. Dane. Reprinted by permission of Random House, Inc.: 14.

From *The Illustrated Life and Times of Wyatt Earp* © 1993 by Bob Boze Bell. Reprinted by permission of Boze Books: 75.

From *I Married Wyatt Earp, The Recollections of Josephine Sarah Marcus Earp* © 1990 by The Arizona Board of Regents, ed. Glenn G. Boyer. Reprinted by permission of University of Arizona Press: 49, 85, 86.

From *The Old-Time Cowhand* © by Ramon F. Adams. Reprinted by permission of Macmillan Publishing Company: 43.

From *The Old West Speaks* © 1956 by Howard R. Driggs. Reprinted by permission of Bonanza Books: 6, 26.

From *Roosevelt in the Bad Lands* © 1921 by Hermann Hagedorn. Reprinted by permission of Houghton Mifflin Company: 2, 19, 23, 40.

From *Saloons of the Old West* © 1979 by Richard Erdoes. Reprinted by permission of Random House, Inc.: 66, 69, 89.

"Speak to Me with Your Hands" © by John Smith. Reprinted by permission of Granada Publishing Ltd.: 32.

From *Tombstone, Myth and Reality* © 1972 by Odie B. Faulk. Reprinted by permission of Oxford University Press: 29, 79.

From *Tombstone's Yesterday: True Chronicles of Early Arizona* © 1968 by Lorenzo D. Walters. Reprinted by permission of Rio Grande Press, Inc.: 63.

From *When Beauty Rode the Rails, An Album of Railroad Yesterdays* © 1962 Lucius Beebe and Charles Clegg. Reprinted by permission of Bantam Doubleday Dell Publishing Group, Inc.: 58.

From *The Wilder Shore: A History of the Gala Days of San Francisco* © 1968 by Stephen Longstreet. Reprinted by permission of Bantam Doubleday Dell Publishing Group, Inc.: 11.

From *Wyatt Earp, Frontier Marshal* © 1955 by Stuart Lake. Reprinted by permission of Houghton Mifflin: 17, 39, 46, 51, 52, 54, 64, 92, 101.

Ben and Jim wish to express their gratitude to Tania Garcia, Esther Margolis, and Keith Hollaman for helping them realize their dream. Special thanks to Kathleen McLaughlin for her countless hours spent researching additional text. Maria Machado proved invaluable coordinating the project.

They would also like to acknowledge the following people for their contributions to the art book: Blanc, Williams, Johnston & Kronstadt, Kevin Costner, Mike Dileonardo, Alan Disler, Magaly Doty, Steve Dunn, Elle Elliott, Grace Farrell, Richard Fezzey, Ian Fox, Joe Gannon, Mike Gannon, Rusty Geller, John Glaeser, Michael Grillo, Michael Harkavy, Norman Howell, Larry Kasdan, Ian Kincaid, Kim Kono, Ian Logan, McCay Accountancy, Moira McLaughlin, Jessie Mesa, Shari Mikulenka, Craig Morton, Richard Mosier, Charlie Okun, Frank Perez, Bill and Victor Petrotta, John Pritchett, Mike Raspa, Danis Regal, Tony Rivetti, Bill Roe, Owen Roizman, Tim Ryan, Sage, Joel Shryack, Diane Sponslor, Spooky Stevens, Caroline Urbas, Dennis Walman, Warner Bros., Lynne Whiteford, Sam Wilson, and all of the *Wyatt Earp* cast and crew.

GENERAL
MERCHAND